Negotiating Skills

How to Negotiate Anything to Your Advantage

Jim Berry

All rights reserved. No part of this publication may be reproduced in any form without written consent of the author and the publisher. The information contained in this book may not be stored in a retrieval system, or transmitted in any form by any means, electronic, mechanical, photocopying or otherwise without the written consent of the publisher. This book may not be resold, hired out or otherwise disposed by way of trade in any form of binding or cover other than that in which it is published, without the written consent of the publisher.

Legal Disclaimer

The information contained in this book is strictly for educational purpose only. The content of this book is the sole expression and opinion of its author and not necessarily that of the publisher. It is not intended to cure, treat, and diagnose any kind of disease or medical condition. It is sold with the understanding that the publisher is not rendering any type of medical, psychological, legal, or any other kind of professional advice. You should seek the services of a competent professional before applying concepts in this book. Neither the publisher nor the individual author(s) shall be liable for any physical, psychological, emotional, financial, or commercial damages, directly or indirectly by the use of this material, which is provided "as is", and without warranties. Therefore, if you wish to apply ideas contained in this book, you are taking full responsibility for your actions.

Table of Contents

1: What is Negotiation?
2: Different Ways of Negotiating
3: Understanding the Other Party's Position
4: Establishing Reasonable Negotiation Goals
5: Setting the Correct Tone for Negotiations
6: Blind Spots in Negotiations
7: How to Negotiate Through an Impasse
8: What If Analysis in Negotiations
9: Dealing with Difficult People
10: How to Deal with Negotiation Loss
Conclusion

Important Insight

Negotiation is a practice that not everyone approves of. There are those who hate it because they think it is too confrontational or simply they don't want to be bothered. They would rather pay the full price than go through the rough road of negotiation.

When purchasing a new or used car, they prefer paying the sticker price as opposed to haggling and seeking for a better bargain. In the event an appliance they have purchased breaks down, they quickly accept that by complaining to the customer service department it won't do them any good. The result of all this is frustration and self-blame.

Looking at negotiation critically, you will discover that there are numerous ways through which you can achieve your goals in negotiation without feeling the weight of anxiety.

This book will show you how negotiations in everyday transactions do not necessarily have to be confrontational, instead they can be fun. You will learn how to avoid destructive arguments in certain situations and still be on course to achieving your goals in the negotiation process.

The guidelines illustrated in this book will teach you a new way of dealing with people regardless of how difficult or insensitive they are. You will become a better negotiator in both the simple and complex day-to-day negotiations that many people fear.

1: What is Negotiation?

It is interesting that it never occurs to many people that the world around us is a negotiating table. Whether you like it or not, you will be drawn into a negotiation of some sort at one point or the other. If you are lucky, you will emerge on the winning side.

At times, things can get ugly making it difficult for you to handle the encounter. In such a circumstance, it becomes almost impossible to get what you want.

A negotiation is defined as a mutual discussion and arrangement of the terms of a transaction or agreement. From this definition, it is clear that one of the key characteristics of a negotiation is the existence of a mutual standing. In short, a negotiation is not meant to be a one-sided affair but rather each of the parties involved is expected to be heard.

Depending on the context, it can be called "dickering over terms" or haggling but one thing remains, the expectation of a give and take between the parties to the negotiation.

There is a common belief that unless you receive everything you are asking for in a negotiation, you are considered a failure. Nothing can be further from the truth because striking a compromise is the likely settlement that is considered fair to each party.

Being rude or overly aggressive does not guarantee you a right of way into forcing the other party to give you what you want. As a matter of fact, any attempt to get everything your way can actually make you end up with less than you would have otherwise received. It is always good to keep in mind that a true negotiation process is bound by compromises and you can't always get what you want.

Some people believe that before the negotiation is concluded, each of the negotiating parties should have received a valuable bargain. This is commonly known as a win-win outcome. While it may be the desired result for all the parties involved, the reality is that more often than not, one party will get more than the other.

Stages in a Negotiation

In order to achieve an outcome that is desirable, it is important that you follow a structured approach to a negotiation. In as much as people suggest different approaches to the negotiation process, there are certain stages that prominently feature in these approaches.

Preparation

Experts in negotiations suggest that you have to be very confident and must have a clear mindset when you get into a negotiation. It is important that you prepare adequately just as it is with any other task. The degree of preparation will determine how far you will go at the negotiating table.

A decision has to be reached beforehand between the negotiating parties as to when and where the meeting will be held and the parties to attend. When you prepare well before the discussion, you will avoid conflict and misunderstandings that amount to a waste of time.

Clarification of Goals

The goals, viewpoints and interests of both sides in a negotiation need to be clarified in order of priority. Such a clarification will help in establishing a common ground. Clarification also prevents misunderstandings which have the potential to cause problems and erect barriers to bar further discussion.

Discussion Stage

At this stage of the negotiation, individuals on either side of the divide put forward their case as per their own understanding. The discussion stage requires skills such as questioning, listening and clarifying. Taking notes at this stage is important because all the points put forward by the other party may require future for clarification. In the negotiation, every side should be given ample time and equal opportunity to present their case.

A win-win outcome is usually the best result in a negotiation. Every party should feel that the negotiation was not in vain and their points of view have been taken into consideration. Even though it may be difficult to attain, a win-win situation should be the ultimate goal of the discussion. In order to arrive at this outcome, alternative strategies and compromises should be considered.

Agreement

An agreement is achieved once the perspectives and interests of each side have been considered. The parties to the negotiation should keep an open mind throughout the discussion so that an acceptable solution can be achieved. The details of every agreement reached should be clear to every side so as to avoid further conflict because of a misunderstanding of the agreement.

Implementing a Course of Action

Once the agreement has been reached and every party is comfortable, a course of action is then implemented to carry through the decision.

Failure to Agree

Should the negotiations break down, the meeting must be rescheduled to a further date. Doing this will prevent the negotiating sides from becoming embroiled in heated arguments which in addition to wasting time can jeopardize future relationships. In the subsequent meetings, the stages of the negotiation process should be repeated and any fresh ideas factored in. It will also help to bring in a third party to mediate the talks.

Informal Negotiations

Not every negotiation goes through the pathway as discussed above. Some follow an informal route which may or may not include the stages as shown above. It must however be emphasized that the key points as expressed in the stages of formal negotiations are critical and should therefore be adhered to.

2: Different Ways of Negotiating

There are different styles of negotiating that people use. Each of these types has a certain impact on the final outcome. Some people prefer quick negotiations while others tend to drag along in reaching an agreement.

Identifying and understanding the different styles of negotiation is very important if you are to get a good bargain out of every negotiation process.

If you are careful enough to take a look around you, you will notice that many people are confident and understand exactly what they want in any situation. As such, they will put forward their opinions, perspectives and interests and will also be willing to hear what the other person has to say.

Being confident about your negotiating style will enable you to face every conflict without fear. As a matter of fact, you will be happy to present your argument at the right time.

The 3Cs of Negotiation Styles

A discussion about negotiation styles cannot be started without mentioning the 3Cs of negotiation styles. These are; Competitive, Collaborative and Concession.

Collaborative Negotiation

This is also referred to as constructive negotiation. Collaborative negotiation singles out and treats the relationship between the negotiating parties as a very valuable and important element. This negotiation style can either resort to a joint problem solving approach or a win-win approach.

In a win-win approach, both parties believe that they have gained something of value at the end of the negotiation process. The result however may not be satisfying because nature has it that we become more comfortable where all our needs are met irrespective of what the other person gets. The win-win approach strikes a compromise and every party has to give in something so as to reach an agreement.

Joint problem solving on the other hand is an approach that can be adopted where the parties to a negotiation are willing to solve the problem at hand. Through this approach, the persons in the argument take an objective-based decision so as to get rid of the issue they are both facing. The disadvantage with this approach is that things may not turn out well especially where the other person sees your willingness to work together as a weakness.

Collaborative approach does not mean that either of the parties is weak. Instead, it is an indication that you want the best possible solution that will make each one of you cheer up at the end of the process.

Competitive Negotiation

As the name suggests, competitive negotiation is a style that treats the entire negotiation process as a competition where one party will emerge the winner while the other the loser. This is why these negotiations tend to be more aggressive and the dealings undertaken in a hard way.

None of the parties care about the relationship at stake but rather each one is concerned with what they will get out of the negotiation. The moment you show any signs of concern for the other person in this kind of negotiation, people immediately assume that you are either weak or you have sinister motives to deceive or defraud. Because of the carefree attitude that every person brings into the negotiating table, competitive negotiations can get really heated.

Those who stick to a competitive approach, usually get assertive and express unwillingness to cooperate. One of the easiest ways to find out whether a party to a negotiation uses this style is by looking at how they turn every situation to their favor and only focus on the issues that matter to them and not the other person. They will do all they can to win the race rather than striving to find an amicable solution.

Concession Negotiation

This type of negotiation is principally different from the collaborative and competitive approach. Here, the parties to the negotiation have lots of consideration for each other. They put themselves at the back and consider others as being very important.

Those who follow this approach tend to prioritize and think more about the needs of the other person. They shelve their own concerns and give them a secondary consideration thereby increasing the chances of ending up with a lose-win situation.

Concession negotiation is commonly interpreted as giving way too much to the other person. People who adopt this style are considered submissive and afraid of conflict.

A Compromise in the Negotiating Styles

Having seen how different each of the negotiating styles is, you could be wondering whether there is a way in between. The good news is that there seems to be a narrow path between collaborative and competitive negotiation.

Here, the parties can act as competitive negotiators where each one of them is racing for the price but still become best friends with the other party the moment the negotiation is concluded. This compromise is commonly seen in political circles where it is said that there are no permanent enemies.

Regardless of your negotiation style, the key to being successful lies in the manner through which you weave your way round to get what you want without being overly aggressive to the other person.

3: Understanding the Other Party's Position

In every negotiation, it is natural that every one of us wants to be the one who is heard the most and who gets the lion share out of the process. This stand point may seem appealing but it can prevent you from listening carefully to the other person and what they have to say. Knowing the position of the other party in the negotiation is extremely important because it is only then that you can strategize on how to make a winning entry.

Learning what the other person is thinking about the subject of the negotiation, gives you a vantage point that you can use to arrive at an amicable solution.

Careful Listening

Many people have been asking the ways through which they can know what the other person is thinking. Well, one of the effective ways you can use is careful listening and paying attention to what they are saying. Remember, thoughts are embodied in words and the more you listen the more you understand the thought process of the other party. There is always a temptation to be more interested in what we have to say other than what the other person is putting across. This is a mistake that can be very costly in negotiations.

Put Yourself in Their Shoes

You should always try to determine what the other person wants to achieve and what it is that they hold so dear that they cannot afford to give it up. Ask yourself throughout the negotiation process, what you would do if you were in your opponent's shoes? This question will help you to get a clear picture from his perspective about the stakes in the negotiation.

Be Observant On the Changing Nature of Issues

One thing you should also be careful about is the changing nature of issues. At the beginning of the negotiation, one issue may be considered more important than the others but along the way, other issues may emerge that take over the negotiation scene. Being alert on these issues will enable you to maintain the tempo throughout the discussion.

People at times confuse power negotiations to mean one party steamrolling over the other. This however should not be the case. Power negotiation is about resolving a problem in the best interests of both parties. It makes a lot of sense to take into account the other party's point of view and appreciating the role that they play in the negotiation.

Pose Open-Ended Questions

During the course of the negotiations, posing open-ended questions can reveal the thought process of the other person. This is because people want to be heard and they can easily reveal their position the moment you give them an opportunity. You do not necessarily have to believe every word they say but you must at least pay attention to what they have to say.

An excellent negotiating technique is to use phrases and words such as '"we" in discussing the subject matter of the negotiation. This type of wording is important in emphasizing that both parties to the negotiation are together in this and they want to find a way of addressing the issue between them. This is particularly the case when the people negotiating have an ongoing relationship such as family members, co-workers or customers. This technique should also be applied in negotiations with parties that you may deal with in future.

The Common Personalities in Negotiations

Each one of us has a unique personality that is often displayed during negotiations. Understanding the position of the other person requires that you know a little bit about their personalities.

There are four different types of personalities and each one corresponds to a different negotiating style. These include dominant, communicator, integrator, and perfectionist.

Dominant Personality

This is the personality of determined people who enjoy being in control of issues. They are stubborn and can be impatient during negotiations. Some individuals with this personality become extremely inflexible and may not listen to what you have to say.

The moment you realize that the other person has this kind of personality, immediately change gears and ask specific questions that are focused more on results. Ensure that you use facts to support your discussion because dominant personalities require a lot of convincing.

At the negotiating table, try as much as possible not to invade their personal space because this can make them agitated.

Communicator Personality

Also known as expressive, communicators are people who are more responsive and enthusiastic about the subject of the discussion. They have flexible agendas and are often willing to listen to your side of the story. Communicators pay more attention to relationships and have the potential to make creative decisions. Expressive negotiators are emotional and therefore you should handle them in a friendly manner.

The Integrator or Amiable Personality

These people are not goal-oriented and their aim is to become everyone's friend. Because of their risk averseness, they depend heavily on the other party so as to reach a decision. It is very easy to find a common ground with such negotiating parties.

Despite their seemingly easy-to-go attitude, dealing with integrator will require that you be patient. They are not a simple pushover because they can take quite some time before agreeing on a solution. You need to stick to your plan and apply some low risk solutions in order to get what you want.

Perfectionist or Analytical Personality

Just as the name suggests, these are people who want everything to be in precise order. They have an enviable control over their behavior and form excellent problem solvers. Despite their rigid requirements, convincing them is rather easy as long as your submission is backed by facts and logic.

One of the easiest ways of negotiating with analytical personalities is to speak less and take more action.

A negotiation being a communication process to help two parties reach a compromise, you need to keep a close eye on your interests as well as those of other person.

4: Establishing Reasonable Negotiation Goals

Before any negotiation, you must formulate what it is that you want to achieve. Setting goals is one of the key principles of good negotiators. Knowing what you want will help you in deploying the right tactics that will achieve the set goal. It does not come as a shock that some people lack a clear understanding of the things they want to accomplish through the negotiation process. They may have a vague idea but not an established goal of where they want to end up.

Each time you negotiate, your eyes should be on the price that you hope to achieve. A famous author, Steven Covey, wrote in his book, "the seven habits of highly effective people," about beginning a process with the end in mind. The reason why this formula works is that having a goal in mind will enable you to negotiate in such a manner as to facilitate the accomplishment of the goal. It does not matter the type of negotiation you are involved in; you could be discussing where to go for dinner or asking for a raise from your boss.

Do not be afraid to express your goal to the other person because failure to communicate can be a major cause of frustration.

How to Decide on Negotiation Goals

Coming up with a goal or a set of goals in a negotiation requires research and planning. Assume you want to buy a new car at the best price possible. When you head to the showroom, you will see the price sticker on the vehicle that you are interested in. (If you are familiar with buying of vehicles, the sticker price is usually the beginning price and not the price you should pay). It is at that point that you engage the sales person and perhaps the manager as well. In order to prepare for the negotiation, you need to know the best price you can possibly get for the car.

One of the ways to find out this information is through research in automobile-oriented directories. This will enable you to know how much the dealer paid for the vehicle and what his mark-up is. When you have this information, you can then confidently walk to the dealer and start the negotiation process. The research will enable you to establish your negotiation goal and thereby push for the best deal from the sales person.

The same strategy can be used in any sort of negotiation. Ensure that you set your goals based on factual and achievable information.

Prioritize Your Objectives

Most negotiations have more than one desired outcome. When you are negotiating terms with a vendor for instance, your main goal may be to get the item at the most convenient price. You may not be concerned about the payment terms. Your vendor on the other hand may want to get funds upfront and therefore seek the best possible payment terms. Prioritizing your goals will enable you to know the objectives that are most important to you and those that you can compromise on.

Tangible versus Intangible

When you are negotiating, you should start with the tangible goals because these matter the most to your business. You can use the smart goal framework to set these goals and measure performance.

Intangible goals though not as pronounced as the tangible ones are also part of negotiations. They are mostly focused on individual and corporate image other than business fundamentals.

For instance, a manager who has previously lost deals with the union may engage in a negotiation with the intangible objective of redeeming his image. He may adopt a confrontational approach to the negotiation so as to prove his point. Also, a company that has had a negative history concerning its corporate citizenship may enter into a negotiation with the local authority in order to enhance its reputation.

Determine Opponents Goals

As part of the goal establishment process, you should focus not only on your own goals but also the goals of your opponent. This will make it easier for you to find a common ground for a win-win outcome. One of the ways of determining what the other party wants is by making two or three offers that emphasize on different aspects and see the one that attracts them.

For instance, if your vendor is more interested in getting upfront payment as opposed to a larger sum that is spread over a long period then you can use this goal to your advantage.

Know Your BATNA (Best Alternative to a Negotiated Agreement)

Enter every negotiation with a full knowledge of the best alternative that you can accept should you miss out on your primary goal. This will help you to decide on your degree of aggressiveness and how firm you can stick to your goals. If you have another interested vendor willing to commit at an attractive price, you can strike a hard bargain with the current vendor. Otherwise, you may have to compromise on your lower priority goals so as to reach an agreement.

In any setup, you should know how far you can stretch and how low you can bend in accepting the proposed terms. Going into a negotiation without goals is like setting out to sail without your radar. You may move but in the wrong direction.

5: Setting the Correct Tone for Negotiations

At the beginning of every negotiation, it is important that you put your best foot forward. Setting the correct tone early on in the discussion tends to soften even the toughest stands of the negotiating parties. It becomes much easier for the other party to cooperate or be willing to compromise when you become polite to them.

One technique that has been known to work well is to begin a negotiation with simple phrase like, "how are you today?" Though it may appear unsettling, this simple statement has an extremely profound effect on the other person.

In phone conversations in particular, service personnel fielding calls from angry customers may use this tactic to ease the pressure and strike a rapport with them. Even though the service personnel may not be directly responsible for the problems the customers are complaining about, setting the correct tone may even out a rather furious tide.

The moment you show the other party that you understand what they are going through and how difficult it is to be in their shoes, they will soften to your advantage.

Treating the other person as you would like to be treated is a golden rule that not only applies to general life encounters but also in negotiations. You will find that the other person will be more responsive and willing to help not only in solving the problem at hand but also willing to do more for you.

Showing that you have an interest in the other party is one of the keys you can use in a negotiation to get what you want. You may never be best friends with the person or may never speak again after the negotiation but showing concern for their interests will go a long way into making your negotiation very simple and full of beneficial compromises.

Interpersonal Skills That Can Help in Setting the Negotiation Mood

In setting the tone for negotiations, interpersonal skills are crucial. They will help you connect with the other negotiating party. Some of the top skills include:

Social Awareness

Understanding the other person's emotions, concerns and needs is very important in the negotiation process. Everyone comes to the negotiating table to further and safeguard their interests. By displaying an interest in their affairs, you will be able to win them over to your side which is a very good strategy to getting what you want in a negotiation.

Understanding the needs of the other party will enable you to effectively communicate in a way that is intended to meet those needs without compromising on yours. As opposed to manipulation which has a negative connotation, social awareness is aimed at building relationships between the negotiating parties.

Problem Analysis and Solving Skills

Understanding the situation surrounding negotiations will give you an upper hand in setting the tone. In negotiations, parties typically fight over peripheral issues rather than the real problem. As the pacesetter to a negotiation, you need to take time to source, identify and quantify all the micro issues that underlie the primary argument. Ensure that you prioritize them and deal with the minor ones first. This will help in creating a more positive environment for the negotiation.

Emotional Control

However emotive the argument may be, try as much as possible to put your reactions under control. By diffusing any prevailing anger, you will have an advantage of conducting the negotiations in a sober and calm atmosphere. Emotional flare ups usually destroy even the slightest advancements towards an agreement. Do not dismiss the emotional needs of the other party in the discussion but rather consider them jointly as if they were your own needs.

Communication

Effective communication in any negotiation can help in connecting you with the other negotiating party. The more you invest in a good communication platform between you and the other person, the more you are likely to reach an agreement faster because the mood will be that of sincerity and honesty. Below are a few rules on communication that will help you in setting the stage for negotiations.

- Organize Your Thoughts

Before the negotiations start, find time to organize your thoughts so that you can convey the right message in a clear and concise manner. If possible, you can have brief notes and a plan of what you are going to say. This will give you confidence and composure as you enter into the negotiation. There is nothing as disarming to your opponent as a composed and relaxed personality. Do not be in a haste to respond to every question but rather take time and where possible, maintain silence.

- Invest in Non-Verbal Communication

It is true that actions speak louder than words. According to experts, 75 percent of communication is non-verbal. What this means to you as a negotiator is that the words you say should be in tandem with your gestures. Any disharmony between the two can create mistrust and send the wrong tone to the other person in the conversation. Let your words and actions mean exactly what you want to express.

- Be Clear in Your Statements

From the onset, clarity of the statements you make will help you in passing your points across as well as setting a professional mood for the negotiations. Use a few words to express what you mean because lengthy and winding explanations do not receive as much attention as concise statements. Oversimplify your message and elaborate during question time.
Before the negotiation, you can practice and repeat your key points again and again until you can do it without any hesitation during the discussion.

Listening Skills

Listening to the other person attentively as they make their points is beneficial in reaching a mutual agreement. Listening is also a sign of respect and the other party will feel that you are giving them the necessary space to outline their points. Ensure that you open your mind to the message being passed across and make a commitment to listen and follow through from the time they start speaking all the way to the end.

When you are listening, you should take note of the facts as well as the feelings. Try the best you can to eliminate distractions and always respond to the other person with questions that stimulate the conversation. Listening and negotiating are close door neighbors and improving the latter requires the input of the former.

Appreciation

More often than not, negotiations involve intimidation because in theory, the aggressive party is said to be the most likely to win the argument. In reality, this may not be the case. Instead of being callous, you need to show appreciation and concern for the other party. Experience shows that people reciprocate such gestures. Appreciation brings an emotional connection that can turn negotiations that would have otherwise been hostile into friendly bargains.

It is therefore, up to you to decide on the mood and tone of the negotiation. In as much as the other person has an influence, your stand and input are very important. If you decide that the discussion is going to be cool and sober, chances are that it will be exactly that. Have it at the back of your mind that you have the potential to direct the negotiations to a successful end.

6: Blind Spots in Negotiations

As you approach a negotiation, it is natural to feel some nagging suspicion and doubt in your thoughts. As a negotiator, it is easier to become completely immersed in the process that you overlook some of your vulnerabilities. Being blind to obstacles that face your opponent in the negotiation can stall a rather straightforward and simple process.

What is a Blind Spot?

A blind spot can be defined as an error in your thought process that keeps you off from seeing the picture from the perspective of the other person. A gap in your research work and a hole in your logic are some of the things that can lead you to an erroneous assumption. In a nutshell, a blind spot occurs when you allow your investment in the negotiating process to blind you from the issues, tactics and strategies that may surface during the negotiating process.

The following are some of the statements that can point towards the existence of blind spots in a negotiator.

- I have made all the connections to the key decision makers and I am 100 percent sure that they will agree to my recommendations.
- I have comprehensively covered all the concerns that the other person may have and I strongly believe that we shall conclude these negotiations and seal the deal faster.
- It seems that everybody is reading from the same page, therefore, this discussion will be straightforward.
- We are the only parties with a logical choice and so they will have no option but to settle on our proposal.

A careful look at these statements reveals a one-sided affirmation that everything is taken care of. While this may give confidence to the negotiator, it also gives rise to the existence of so many blind spots that can ruin the negotiation process. It is until these statements are subjected to the opinion and perspective of the other party in the negotiation that you will be able to see the deficiencies that lie within them.

Negotiation Blind Spots that Can Ruin the Deal

The Rapport Blind Spot

Striking a rapport with your negotiating partner is excellent and can help you establish the right mood for the discussion. However, you should not confuse a rapport with trust. It is easier to assume that as long as the parties to a negotiation have built a strong rapport, they will automatically trust one another.

The reality is that the other person may like you and even enjoy your company but not trust you. Rapport gives you access but it does not bring out clearly your overall capabilities, the veracity of your pledge to deliver, or the performance of your solution.

Trust embodies credibility and the assurance that the solution you propose will deliver the desired results. It is therefore important to test whether you have built only a rapport or have also developed credibility necessary for the other party to trust you. One of the ways of assessing this is by requesting the other person to share their priorities. Disclosure is very critical and therapeutic to both of you.

Ensure that you reinforce your credibility at every point in the discussion. If you are negotiating with a customer, share results from sales of similar commodities and remind him of your business case and the returns to be expected. Do not focus on worst case scenarios but be ready to add precautionary measures where appropriate.

Corporate Benefits Override Personal Fears

Every investment represents a certain change to the organization. If the investment is complex in nature, the need for change becomes greater. Whether it is an enterprise resource planning software or a machine, the impact goes beyond the organizational level to individual circles.

People perceive change differently. While some see success, others perceive failure at a personal level. It doesn't matter how extraordinary your part of the bargain is, fears and concerns will always rise and influence the buying decision.

Therefore, in a negotiation, it is easier to assume that as long as you are offering something of value, the other person should have no reason to object. This is a blind spot that can potentially kill negotiations and rob you of a lucrative deal.

To get the most out of each negotiation, you need to ask the other person in an honest manner whether any of the things you have discussed and agreed upon make them uncomfortable. By addressing personal concerns of the negotiating party, you are likely to receive an all-round acceptance.

Agreement Means Commitment Blind Spot

In negotiations, not everything that is agreed upon carries an equal measure of commitment. Remember, an agreement requires the input of the other party which could even be a team of stakeholders. The blind spot here occurs when you confuse agreement to mean commitment.

Your task as a negotiator goes beyond a mere agreement. You need to create a heightened commitment that will see the agreement turned into action. It is only by getting a firm commitment from the other party you can consider the negotiations successful.

One way in which you can secure commitment from your negotiating partner is by conducting a controlled discussion. Use a priority sequence to rank the issues to be discussed from the most important to the least.

Thereafter, conduct brainstorming sessions so as to identify possible options. Focus on the urgent issues and request for immediate action and support. Utilize the time in the negotiation process to access the level of commitment from the other party while giving them space to voice their reservations.

Remember, negotiations are about giving and receiving. You should come to the negotiation table prepared to give concessions in as much as you push your own agenda. Come with the right attitude and always maintain an open mind to accept and analyze ideas put forward by the other person. There is more than one way of dealing with a problem and therefore you need to listen carefully to your counterpart's ideas and respond appropriately.

7: How to Negotiate Through an Impasse

Despite the fact that the negotiating parties have common interests, differences in opinions and objectives do emerge thereby creating a deadlock. An impasse is one of the most undesirable aspects to negotiations because it can derail and even stall the process completely.

At the beginning, each of the parties is optimistic that negotiation is one of the ways to solve the differences between them. However as the process gathers steam, you become more tempted to maintain your stand and try to push the other person to change theirs.

As discussed earlier in negotiation planning, you need to have alternatives that you can pursue in the event things do not go your way. A deadlock is one of those events that require you to look at your alternative plans carefully.

Understanding the Causes of Deadlocks

Deadlocks during negotiations arise due to various reasons. Some of the causes may be seen as being unreasonable but the bottom-line is that they have the power to ruin the entire process.

Difference in Objectives

This is the number one reason why people hit snags in negotiations. Everyone has their own objectives that they want to achieve in the discussion. These objectives are often competing and as such, each party tries as much as possible to push their agenda forward. This has the potential of causing a deadlock in the negotiation.

Rigidity of One Party

If one of the parties becomes rigid, the possibility of reaching a conclusive end in the negotiation goes down. Some negotiating partners may be hell-bent in making the negotiations stall purely for selfish reasons. Unless an alternative tactic is embraced, deadlocks can be very challenging and frustrating.

Breaking from these negotiation barriers needs a proper plan. Experts in negotiation matters suggest that before you get into any negotiation, you should already have a backup plan in mind. This is commonly referred to as the plan B. Below are some tips that can go a long way into helping you resolve a problematic situation.

- Identify whether the basis of your disagreement is good or bad.
- Figure out the potential loss that you may suffer if you do not reach an agreement.

- Find out whether the impasse has the potential of cutting out future opportunities with the negotiating party.
- Identify whether there is any other point you can agree on.

Once you figure out the options available, you should then develop a list of actions that you may take if no agreement is reached. Try to use more promising ideas and shape them into practical alternatives that you can use.

One thing that you need to be aware of in negotiations is that positive moods increase the chances of positive results.

If you are in a good mood, you will be able to analyze the implications of not reaching an agreement with a lot of sobriety. A good negotiator always tries to solve the minor problems first so as to avoid a deadlock in the major decision items.

How to Avoid an Abrupt End to Negotiations

As earlier pointed out, you have a role to play in ensuring that the negotiations continue seamlessly with minimal or no hitches at all. Below are some of the things you can do to ensure continuity.

Avoid Direct Confrontation

There is always a temptation to take on the other person in a confrontation duel. This is because some of the statements being made may not go well with you. However much you may be justified, try not to get into arguments. Confrontations never help to solve a situation but rather they amplify and worsen an already bad situation.

Always Listen to the Other Person

Listening in a negotiation is more important than plain talking. Most of the deadlocks that arise during discussions are due to poor listening skills. According to experts, it pays to listen to what the other side is saying because it can help you to adjust your strategy and change your plan so as to achieve a successful result.

Best listeners always prove to be the best negotiators. Through attentive listening, you will be able to read non-verbal clues from your opponent and understand the motive behind the facial expressions, gestures and the tone that the other person uses.

Take Small Breaks to Consolidate Your Thoughts

Whenever the negotiating table becomes heated up, it is important that you take small breaks so as to gather your thoughts and rephrase your questions. As it is with any sort of argument, there is usually hostility in the atmosphere and this can scatter your thoughts making your arguments ineffective. Taking five or ten minute breaks can help you ease out and relax before coming back into the negotiation.

Watch the Language that You Use

The words you use can either build or demolish the negotiations. Harsh words tend to send a message that you are being hostile and as such not ready to negotiate. In order to continue with the negotiations in a smooth manner, try to use a language that is friendly and accommodating. Also, address the concerns of the other party while pushing your own.

For instance, if you do not agree with a point that has been put forward, you can say something like "can you please clarify" or "I am afraid this may not be feasible". Do not be overly aggressive and make statements like "you are wrong" or "this is unfair".

Some negotiators lose their cool and make some outrageous statements that they drive the conversation to a deeper end of the deadlock instead of solving the problem. Remember that in a deadlock, you should look for solutions not complicating the situation further.

Depending on the level of negotiation that you are in, a polite statement could be what is needed to unlock the impasse. You should exercise care when handling a deadlock because without knowing you may give too much information to the other side which may not necessary be needed.

Take your time and come up with a solution that suits your interests as well as the concerns of the other party. You should always be optimistic and know that there is an answer to every problem that you face in the negotiation process.

8: What If Analysis in Negotiations

Every negotiation process has its own unique scenarios that it poses to the participants. As a good negotiator, you should analyze the possible scenarios beforehand in order to come up with tentative responses to each one of them. Some of the common scenarios that may arise include:

The Other Side Is Acting Too Smart

The other party being too rigid or overly smart is one of the challenges that you have to overcome in a negotiation. It is common to come across opponents who may try to intimidate or pressurize you into accepting their points of view. Usually, such people tend to show how clueless you are in the matter being discussed. In the face of all this, there are a few things that you need to keep in mind. It does not matter how smart or rigid your opponent is, there is a chance to convince them in the course of the process.

Handling negotiators who are smart is not an easy task but it does not harm to face them anyway. Speak softly and take short pauses every time they finish talking. Try to overcome your emotional challenges first in order to make yourself stable.

Smart negotiators will press your "Hot Buttons" with an aim of making you to explode and turn the argument in their favor. People act smart for a variety of reasons and at times they do this to give mixed signals in order confuse you. Some of them do it to disguise their negotiation style so that you do not understand them and therefore becoming disadvantaged. Whatever the case, preparing for the unexpected situation beforehand can give you a smart edge over them.

There is Too Much Risk

If you have been through a negotiation process before, you may be aware that such processes are usually uncertain and therefore risky. The question that you should ask yourself is, "how much risk should I take?" Taking risks in negotiations could be as simple as asking for a bigger bargain more than what you know you can get.

Before assuming any risk in a negotiation, always find out the level of risk that is justifiable in the case at hand. Below are a few questions that can be of help as you assess the negotiation risk.

How much risk can you comfortably handle?

Different people have different risk appetites and as such, knowing the risk level that you can accommodate is important. Taking more than you can handle can expose you to unfortunate events.

What alternatives do you have if the negotiation goes the other way?

Not every negotiation works to your favor and some can go the other way. In assessing your risk appetite, you should consider this side of the negotiation and analyze the options that you have.

What if your plan B does not live to your expectations?

Plan B is the fallback strategy to use when your primary plan doesn't succeed. However slim it may be, you should also consider the possibility of the plan B not meeting your expectations 100 percent. What you need to ask yourself is, "in case the plan B fails too, what will I be left with?"

What is of importance here is to remember that all successful negotiators are willing to take certain levels of risk based on logical factors.

You Cannot Handle the Pressure

Your tolerance level can be a barrier in the negotiation process. Each one of us has their own threshold within which we are happy, sad or angry. When these levels are exceeded, there is an almost automatic response that changes our moods.

Remaining resilient under pressure is one of the most valuable qualities of a skilled negotiator. It will enable you to counter every trick in the book that your opponent uses to sway the negotiation to his favor. If you want to be part of the league of skilled negotiators, you have to learn how to stand firm irrespective of how tough the negotiation seems to be. It is your resilience and firm stand that will help you to overcome all the possible barriers and move a step closer towards a successful outcome.

Successful negotiators do not attach themselves to a specific result. This is because such an attachment may cause them to be emotionally involved and eventually give hurried and irrational decisions. In a nutshell, you have to remain in control of your emotions at all times in the course of the negotiation process.

It takes only one emotional slip to cause you to succumb to pressure and eventually detach yourself from the negotiation process.

Walking Away from the Negotiation

Sitting through a negotiation successfully is the desire of every negotiator, you included. It is only then that you can reach an amicable solution. However, the reality on the ground may at times be different from the envisioned process forcing you to walk away from the deal.

No single negotiation process is an exact replica of another. At times, you might feel that things are not working right but unsure of when and how to walk out of the discussion. A common kneejerk reaction which is also one of the biggest mistakes that negotiators can make is leaving the negotiation table abruptly. In as much as the walk away alternative is a powerful tool to sideline your opponent, you have to use it carefully.

Walk away from the negotiation if you have a backup plan or an alternative option that does not require the input of the other person. Also, in instances where your plan B meets your objectives and goals better than the proposed solutions, you may walk out. Never tolerate the use of corrupt, unfair or rude tactics by your opponent.

Before you walk out of the deal, try all the possible ways of reaching an agreement. Let this be the last option after every single approach has hit a dead end.

Where Your Opponent Deviates from the Subject Matter

The negotiation subject or issue is the principle reason why each party makes an offer to the other. If there is no discussion on the subject then it becomes pointless to negotiate. At times, your opponent may shift your focus from the core discussion particularly where they sense defeat. What you need to understand is that in the absence of clear objectives, you can never reach a conclusive end.

Try to convince your opponent and bring them back to the main discussion area. Be clear to them with regards to the objectives and what it is at stake in the negotiation. If things do not work out and your opponent is not willing to cooperate, you can step out of the negotiation.

9: Dealing with Difficult People

Learning to negotiate is an essential human relation and communication skill that you need to master if you are to achieve personal and business success. Not all negotiations will involve friendly persons. In some instances, you will encounter people or organizations that are reluctant to change, therefore requiring tactical approaches into reaching an agreement. Below are some tips you can use to negotiate with difficult people.

Find Out What Makes Them Difficult

In order to deal with your opponent effectively, get to know why they are being difficult. Find out whether their behavior stems from a cultural tendency or trait, a personality style, a specific negotiation tactic or something that happened in their life. Once you know the reason why they are being difficult, you can then devise an approach that will help you deal with them effectively.

To find out these reasons, you can ask them directly or contact other people that have previously dealt with them. You can also lighten the mood with humor and try to build a rapport with them. This can diffuse the difficult elements and get them to open up.

Have a Positive Attitude

The attitude you have when getting into a negotiation will determine the outcome that you will get. If you approach the discussion as an opportunity to achieve a win-all outcome, you may be disappointed and experience resistance from the other party. To get the most, you need to be positive and appreciate the contribution of the other person. Look at the result from the perspective of a mutual benefit.

Meet on a Comfortable and Convenient Ground

Where to meet for your negotiations can also influence the behavior and perspective of the other person. The place must not be seen as being advantageous to one party because this can increase the level of difficulty in the other person. Ensure that you meet in a mutually agreeable location and time. Prepare adequately for the one-on-one meeting and be careful on the way you use your voice and facial expressions because this can ruin your verbal communication.

Define the Issue and Do Your Homework

The subject of discussion must be agreed beforehand by all parties so that you can assess the possible solutions as you plan for the meeting. You need to know what is at stake and also the concerns and motivations of the other party. Categorize your items into two main groups; the negotiable and non-negotiable. Also, determine the best, the fair and the minimally acceptable deal.

Understand Your Opponent and Yourself

When negotiating with difficult people, you have to steer clear of emotions and only deal with the facts of the case. Determine when it is appropriate and how to pass on your points so as to get an effective reception from the other person. Understand the level of trust in the other person and be conscious of the aspects of their personality that can hinder the negotiation process. Never attack or pass judgment to the other person.

Look for Any Shared Interests

Establishing common objectives and goals can help you in setting a ground upon which to base your negotiations. Focus not only at the present but also at the future and discuss what needs to be done and tackle the problem through a collaborative approach. It is very unlikely that the negotiation will lack a common ground or interest.

Exercise Honesty

Difficult situations and people require a very high degree of honesty. Do not try to trick the other person into accepting a certain line of argument but rather be clear about what you consider as important to you. Discuss in an open manner why your goals, objectives and issues are important to you and at the same time show understanding of the issues raised by the other person. Where honesty and openness prevails, trust thrives.

Present Options and Alternatives

Do not be stiff and uncompromising when dealing with a difficult person. This is because such a stand will further stifle the process and jeopardize any chances of reaching an agreement. Coming up with suitable options, is a demonstration of your willingness to compromise in the discussion.

You may also consider giving in on areas that may have perceived value to the other party but not very important to you. When you are framing your options, have the other person's perspective and interests in mind. Always provide evidence and facts for your points of view.

Apply Expert Communication Skills

To handle difficult people in negotiations, you have to employ tactical communication skills. Ask questions to keep the conversation going, listen carefully and rephrase what you have heard so as to clarify your understanding and show interests in the concerns of the other party.

Try to reduce tension through humor and give space to the other party to air their views. Do not focus too much on your position but rather shift your focus and dwell more on the ways through which you can move forward into a resolution.

End on a Win-Win Note

The end of the negotiation is as important as the beginning. Ensure that every party to the deal feels that they have achieved something of value. Agree on the implementation process and the people responsible for handling each step. This will make it easy to win over even the most difficult people.

10: How to Deal with Negotiation Loss

Defeat is never admirable in any context including negotiations. There is an argument that negotiators never lose but rather they get something lesser than they expected. Whatever the case may be, defeat is part and parcel of negotiations.

When you come to the negotiation table, there are certain goals that you would like to achieve. The other party also has their own set of goals and objectives which in most cases are not congruent with yours. Learning to accept defeat and moving on is a commendable character that not everyone has.

It is often said that you can judge the character of a person by the way they respond to loss and defeat. Below are five ways through which you can handle defeat gracefully.

Accept It

It is never easy to acknowledge and accept negotiation loss but the only option to get out of the feeling is to accept it. Just know that it has already happened and there is no point in crying over spilt milk. Acceptance gives you the power to reduce the impact of the loss to a few days or hours. Remember that not all negotiations go in your favor and you are not the only one who walks that path.

Learn From It

Loss is not equal to failure irrespective of how close the two are. In fact, any notion that bundles up the two in one basket is erroneous and misleading. Accept the loss as a challenge and quickly learn from the things you did or did not do so as to better your craft. Competition is never about other people but rather about your potential to succeed. You should interpret the negotiation loss as a wakeup call to improve your abilities and not the final nail on your coffin.

Move Forward

Do not dwell on what did not go your way but instead set your focus on a new goal and pursue it with all your might. Create new challenges that will push you to another level. If you feel that you lost because you had taken a much bigger objective or goal, set your sight on smaller goals that will ultimately build up to the bigger picture. Every accomplished journey is a series of small steps; therefore keep moving.

Emulate Your Role Models

In every situation in life including negotiations, you require role models that you can look up to. Whether it is a business deal or a personal negotiation, find out how your role models went through a similar experience and how they dealt with the loss thereafter.

There is a very high likelihood that the approaches they used could also work for you. Do not be shy or indignant to discuss with them the things you are going through. There is never a situation that is unique to you, and what you are going through is something that another person experienced at some point in their lives. Seek for solutions not excuses.

Shift Your Attention

Following a negotiation loss, instances of self-doubt and negativity may occupy your mind and constantly inject feelings of ineptitude into your emotions. Entertaining such thoughts can have negative implications on you and even affect the quality of your life.

To move from this setup, you need to deliberately shift your attention to something else. You can even engage in an activity that is totally unrelated to the negotiations that you had. This positive distraction will give you space for healing and an opportunity to move on.

Handle new negotiations with a new stream of energy and optimism believing that you have a chance to prove your worth once more.

Conclusion

Becoming a master negotiator therefore requires that you develop certain qualities such as problem solving abilities, confidence and the flexibility to change tactic during the negotiation process. Practice always makes perfect and the more time and resources you put into the negotiation planning, the higher the chances that you will succeed and get what you want.

Remember that you are not the only one on the negotiation table but rather a party to a wide range of interests and perspectives. Try to accommodate the views and concerns of the other people by listening carefully to what they are saying. You will be amazed at how they yield to your demands and feel your commitment.

Build your arguments on facts and always ask questions that portray your interest on the issue being negotiated on. Clarify every idea being put across so that you do not assume that a point is clear while it is not. Do not try to win every argument because this can make you look aggressive and rude from the perspective of your opponent. On the contrary, strive to make your argument reasonable and fair across the board.

In a negotiation process, every person is significant and there is no ultimate decision maker. Do not dictate what needs to be done and the perspective to be followed. Instead, win people over to your side through the simple tactic of communication skills. Be open to positive criticism and do not take anything personal. Being calm and composed will position you at a vantage point to win any negotiation.

www.ingramcontent.com/pod-product-compliance
Lightning Source LLC
Chambersburg PA
CBHW071812170526
45167CB00003B/1286